Teach Your Cat
MANX

If you're going to teach your (or someone else's) cat a little Manx (and why wouldn't you?), this is the ideal place to start.

Funny & surprisingly clever books. Love. Love.

Anne Cakebread not only has the best name in the Universe, she has also come up with a brilliantly fun book.

A purrfectly delightful book.

Teach Your Cat

MANX

Anne Cakebread

Thank you to:
Helen, Marcie, Frieda, Lily and Nina, my
family, friends and neighbours in St Dogmaels
for all their support and encouragement. Adrian
Cain, Manx Language Officer at Culture Vannin,
Carolyn at Y Lolfa and Chris Sheard for Manx
translations and pronunciations.
Gura mie eu.

First impression 2020

Illustrations and design by Anne Cakebread

ISBN: 978-1-78461-831-5

Published and printed in Wales on paper from well-maintained forests by Y Lolfa Cyf., Talybont, Ceredigion SY24 5HE
e-mail ylolfa@ylolfa.com
website www.ylolfa.com
tel 01970 832 304
fax 832 782

Teach
Your Cat
Manx

"Hello"

"Laa mie"

pron:
"Lair my"

"Come here"

"Tar hym"

pron:

"T<u>a</u>r hum"

'ar'
as in
'b<u>ar</u>rel'

"Leave it!"

"Faag eh!"

pron:

"Fairg _ay!_"

'ay'
as in
's_ay_'

"Don't!"

"Ny jean!"

pron:
"**Ner** jin!"

'Ner'
as in
'ru**nner**'

"No!"

"Scuirr!"

pron:
"Skwir!"

"Very good"

"Feer vie"

pron:
"Fee vie"

'ie'
as in
'pie'

"How much is it?"

"Quoid t'eh costal?"

pron:

"Kwud tay costal?"

'u'
as in
'put'

"Don't scratch"

"Ny screeb"

pron:

"**Ner** screeb"

'Ner'
as in
'ru**nner**'

"Are you OK?"

"Vel oo kiart
dy liooar?"

pron:
"Vell oo k'yart
the l'yewer?"

"Bedtime"

"Traa goll dy lhie"

pron:

"Trair goll the lie"

'air'
as in
'hair'

"Goodnight"

"Oie vie"

pron:

"Ee vie"

'ie'
as in
'pie'

"Quiet!"

"Gow-jee fea!"

pron:
"G<u>ow</u>-jee fay!"

'ow'
as in
'c<u>ow</u>'

"Good morning"

"Moghrey mie"

pron:
"Morra my"

"What's the time?"

"Cre'n traa t'eh?"

pron:
"Kren trair tay?"

'air' as in 'hair'

"Lunchtime"

"Traa kirbyl"

pron:

"Trair kerble"

'air'
as in
'hair'

"Are you full?"

"Vel oo lane?"

pron:

"Vell oo le<u>d</u>n?"

barely
pronounce
this 'd'

"All gone"

"Ooilley eeit"

pron:
"Ool-yew yee-itch"

"It's warm"

"T'eh blah"

pron:
"Tay _blah_"

'bla'
as in
'_bla_ck',
with the 'a'
drawn out

"It's snowing"

"T'eh ceau sniaghtey"

pron:

"Tay k'yow sn'yachter"

'ow' as in 'cow'

'ch' as in 'Loch Ness'

"It's cold"

"T'eh feayr"

pron:
"Tay fooer"

"It's hot"

"T'eh çheh"

pron:
"Tay chay"

"It's raining"

"T'eh ceau fliaghey"

pron:
"Tay k'yow fl'ya"

'ow' as in 'cow'

"It's windy"

"T'eh geayagh"

pron:
"Tay gaya_ch_"

'ch'
as in
'Lo_ch_
Ness'

"It's sunny"

"T'eh grianagh"

pron:

"Tay greer-nach"

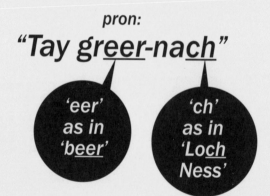

'eer'
as in
'beer'

'ch'
as in
'Loch
Ness'

"Come down"

"Tar neose"

pron:

"T<u>ar</u> no-ss"

'ar'
as in
'b<u>ar</u>rel'

"Do you want to play?"

"Mie lhiat cloie?"

pron:

"My l'yat clie?"

'ie'
as in
'pie'

"football"

"bluckan-coshey"

pron:
"bluggan-c<u>aw</u>zh<u>e</u>r"

'aw'
as in
'p<u>aw</u>'

'zh'
as in
'<u>Zh</u>ivago'

"What have you got?"

"C'red t'ayd?"

pron:

"Ki<u>rru</u>d ted?"

'irru'
as in
'sti<u>rru</u>p'

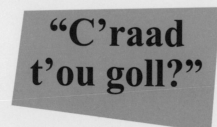

"Where are you going?"

"C'raad t'ou goll?"

pron:
"Crared tow goll?"

'ow' as in 'cow'

'ared' as in 'shared'

"What have you been doing?"

"Cre v'ou jannoo?"

pron:

"Kre vow jinnoo?"

'e' as in 'met'

'ow' as in 'cow'

emphasise this syllable

"headache"

"çhingys-king"

pron:

"ch<u>ing</u>us-king"

'ing'
as in
'fi<u>ng</u>er'

"Have you got
tummy ache?"

"Vel
çhingys-bolg
ayd?"

pron:

"Vell
chingus-bulg
ed?"

'ing'
as in
'finger'

"Have you got a cold?"

"Vel feayraght ort?"

pron:

"Vell foo-ra<u>ch</u>t art?"

'ch'
as in
'Lo<u>ch</u>
Ness'

"Where are you?"

"C'raad t'ou?"

pron:

"Crared tow?"

'ared'
as in
'shared'

'ow'
as in
'cow'

"Don't be afraid"

"Ny bee aggle ort"

pron:

"_Ner_ bee _al_ art"

'Ner'
as in
'run_ner_'

'al'
as in
'can_al_'

"Get out!"

"Magh lhiat!"

pron:

"Mach l'yat!"

'ch'
as in
'Loch
Ness'

"Is that your favourite toy?"

"Nee shen y gaih share lhiat?"

pron:

"Nay shen <u>er</u> guy-ee share l'yat?"

'er' as in 'din<u>ner</u>'

"Do you
want a cuddle?"

"Mie lhiat
nuiddragh?"

pron:
"My l'yat
noo-drach?"

'ch'
as in
'Loch
Ness'

"Cheers!"

"Slaynt vie!"

pron:

"Slent vie!"

'ie'
as in
'pie'

"I love you"

"Shynney
lhiam oo"

pron:
"Shinner
I'yam oo"

"Happy Birthday"

"Laa Ruggyree Sonney"

pron:
"Lair Ruggeree Sonner"

"Good luck"

"Aigh vie"

pron:

"Aych vie"

'Ay'
as in
'say'

'ch'
as in
'Loch
Ness'

'ie'
as in
'pie'

"Merry Christmas"

"Nollick Ghennal"

pron:

"Nollig Yennal"

'al' as in 'petal'

"Happy New Year!"

"Blein Vie Noa!"

pron:
"Blane Vie No!"

'ie'
as in
'pie'

"Thank you"

"Gura mie ayd"

pron:

"Gurrer my ed"

"How many?"

"Cre whilleen?"

pron:

"Kre hwill'yin?"

'e'
as in
'met'

1 one

"un"

pron:
"un"

'un'
as in
'<u>un</u>do'

2 two

"daa"

pron:
"dare"

3
three
"three"
pron:
"tree"

4
four
"kiare"
pron:
"k'yair"

5
five
"queig"
pron:
"kwegg"

6
six
"shey"
pron:
"shay"

9
nine
"nuy"
pron:
"na-ee"

10
ten
"jeih"

pron:
"ja-ee"

20
twenty
"feed"

pron:
"feed"

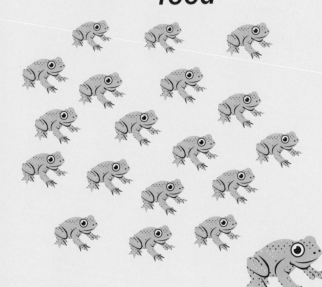

100
one hundred

"keead"

pron:

"keed"

"Are you happy?"

"Vel oo maynrey?"

pron:

"Vell oo man-rer?"

'a' as in 'p<u>a</u>n' but with the 'a' more drawn out

'rer' as in 'ca<u>rer</u>'

"Have you got
enough room?"

"Vel reamys
dy liooar ayd?"

pron:
"Vell raymus
the l'yewer ed?"

"Goodbye"

"Slane lhiat"

pron:
"Sle_d_n l'yat"

barely
pronounce
this 'd'

Other titles in this series include:

Teach Your Cat Welsh
Teach Your Dog Welsh
Teach Your Dog Cornish
Teach Your Dog Gaelic
Teach Your Dog Irish
Teach Your Dog Māori
and
Teach Your Dog Japanese
Rugby World Cup 2019 Travel Edition

www.ylolfa.com